POWER PLAYS
THE NEXT 100 YEARS OF ENERGY

by Nikole Brooks Bethea

CAPSTONE PRESS
a capstone imprint

Graphic Library is published by Capstone Press,
1710 Roe Crest Drive, North Mankato, Minnesota 56003
www.mycapstone.com

Library of Congress Cataloging-in-Publication data is available on the Library of Congress website.
ISBN 978-1-4914-8267-4 (library binding)
ISBN 978-1-4914-8271-1 (eBook PDF)

Editor
Mandy Robbins

Art Director
Nathan Gassman

Designer
Ted Williams

Media Researcher
Jo Miller

Production Specialist
Katy LaVigne

Illustrator
Alan Brown

Colorist
Sara Foresti

Design Element: Shutterstock: pixelparticle (backgrounds)

Printed and bound in the United States of America.
009679F16

TABLE OF CONTENTS

SECTION ONE ENERGY PAST AND PRESENT

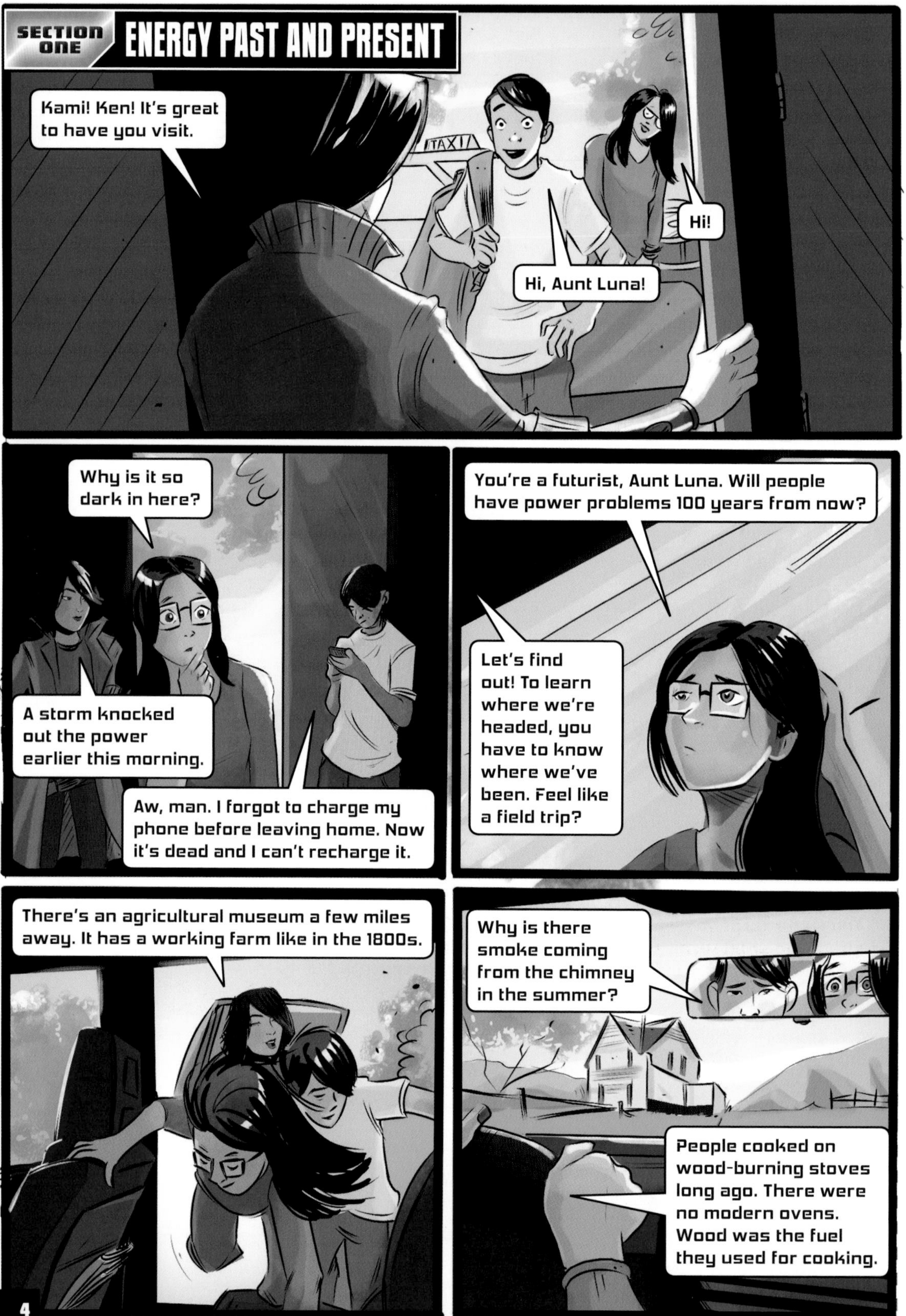

Kami! Ken! It's great to have you visit.
TAXI
Hi, Aunt Luna!
Hi!
Why is it so dark in here?
A storm knocked out the power earlier this morning.
Aw, man. I forgot to charge my phone before leaving home. Now it's dead and I can't recharge it.
You're a futurist, Aunt Luna. Will people have power problems 100 years from now?
Let's find out! To learn where we're headed, you have to know where we've been. Feel like a field trip?
There's an agricultural museum a few miles away. It has a working farm like in the 1800s.
Why is there smoke coming from the chimney in the summer?
People cooked on wood-burning stoves long ago. There were no modern ovens. Wood was the fuel they used for cooking.

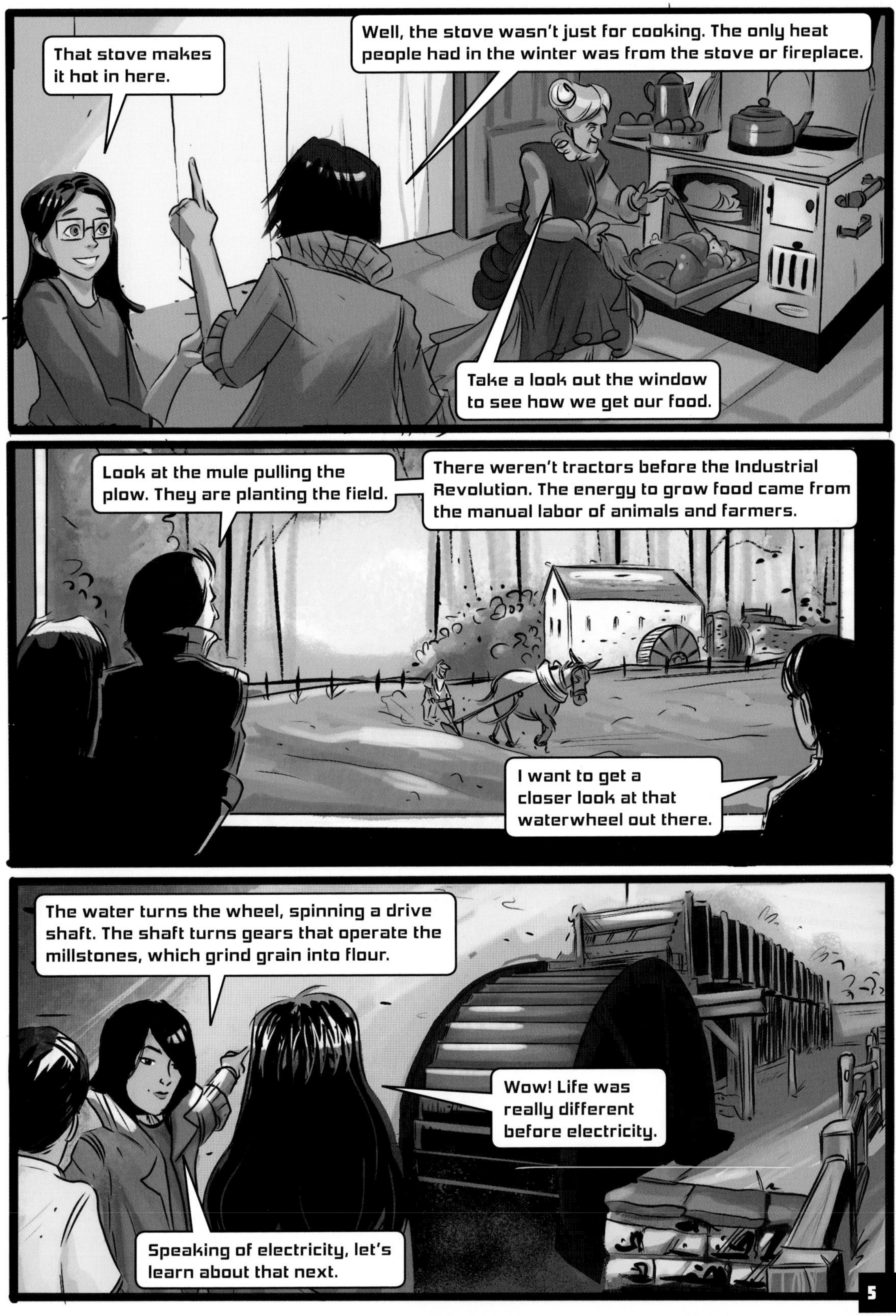
That stove makes it hot in here.
Well, the stove wasn't just for cooking. The only heat people had in the winter was from the stove or fireplace.
Take a look out the window to see how we get our food.
Look at the mule pulling the plow. They are planting the field.
There weren't tractors before the Industrial Revolution. The energy to grow food came from the manual labor of animals and farmers.
I want to get a closer look at that waterwheel out there.
The water turns the wheel, spinning a drive shaft. The shaft turns gears that operate the millstones, which grind grain into flour.
Wow! Life was really different before electricity.
Speaking of electricity, let's learn about that next.

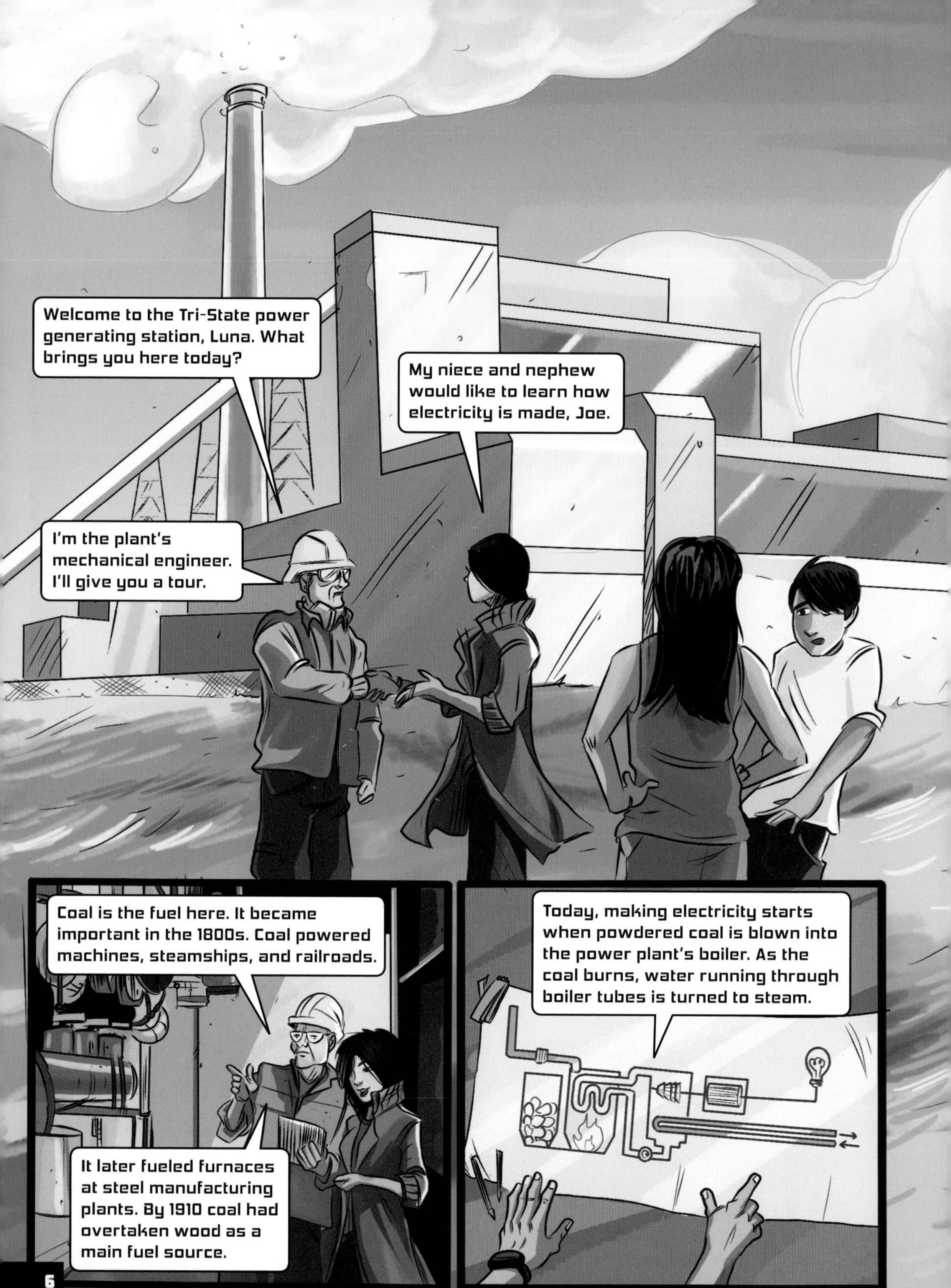
Welcome to the Tri-State power generating station, Luna. What brings you here today?
My niece and nephew would like to learn how electricity is made, Joe.
I'm the plant's mechanical engineer. I'll give you a tour.
Coal is the fuel here. It became important in the 1800s. Coal powered machines, steamships, and railroads.
It later fueled furnaces at steel manufacturing plants. By 1910 coal had overtaken wood as a main fuel source.
Today, making electricity starts when powdered coal is blown into the power plant's boiler. As the coal burns, water running through boiler tubes is turned to steam.

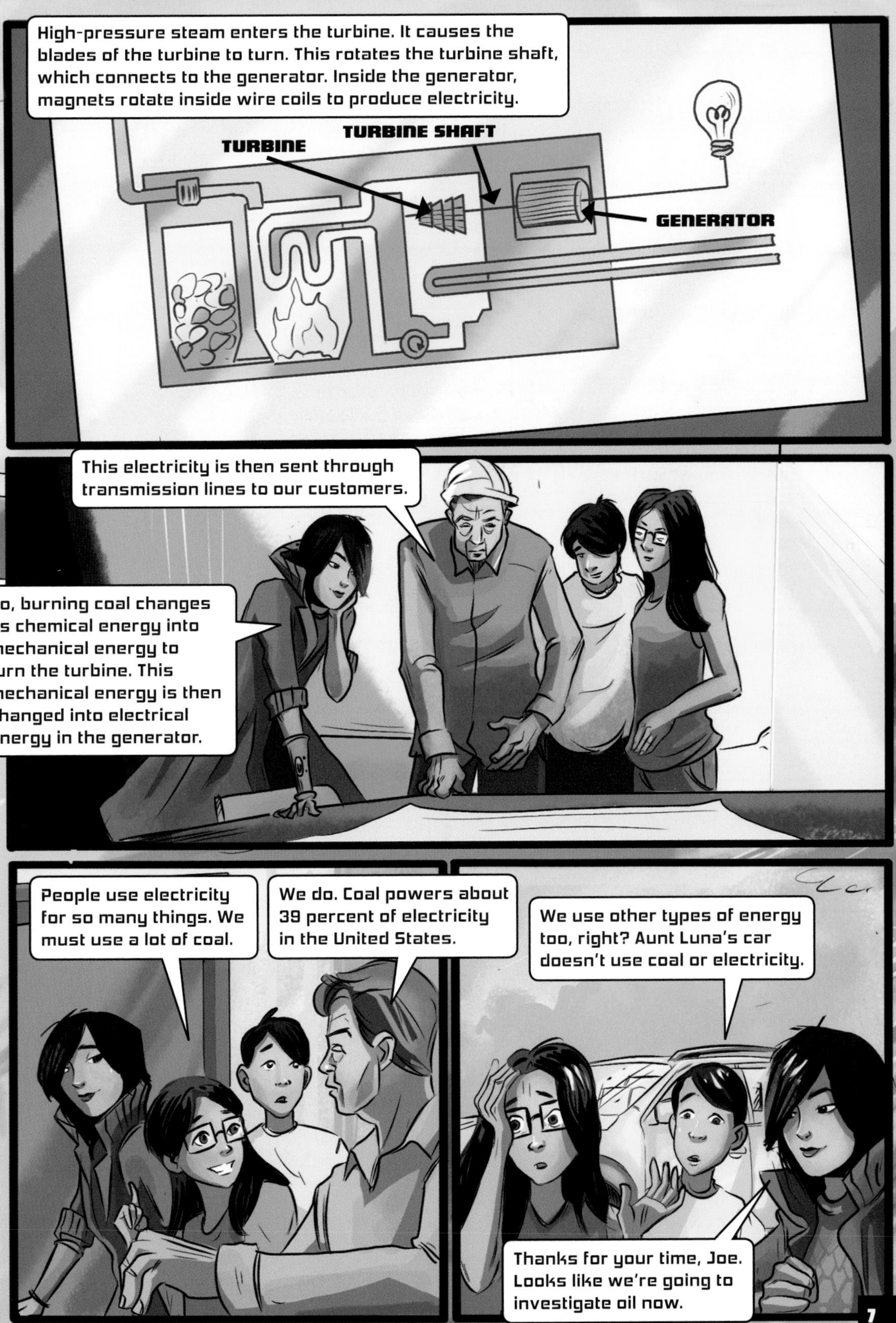
High-pressure steam enters the turbine. It causes the blades of the turbine to turn. This rotates the turbine shaft, which connects to the generator. Inside the generator, magnets rotate inside wire coils to produce electricity.
TURBINE SHAFT
TURBINE
GENERATOR
This electricity is then sent through transmission lines to our customers.
So, burning coal changes its chemical energy into mechanical energy to turn the turbine. This mechanical energy is then changed into electrical energy in the generator.
People use electricity for so many things. We must use a lot of coal.
We do. Coal powers about 39 percent of electricity in the United States.
We use other types of energy too, right? Aunt Luna's car doesn't use coal or electricity.
Thanks for your time, Joe. Looks like we're going to investigate oil now.

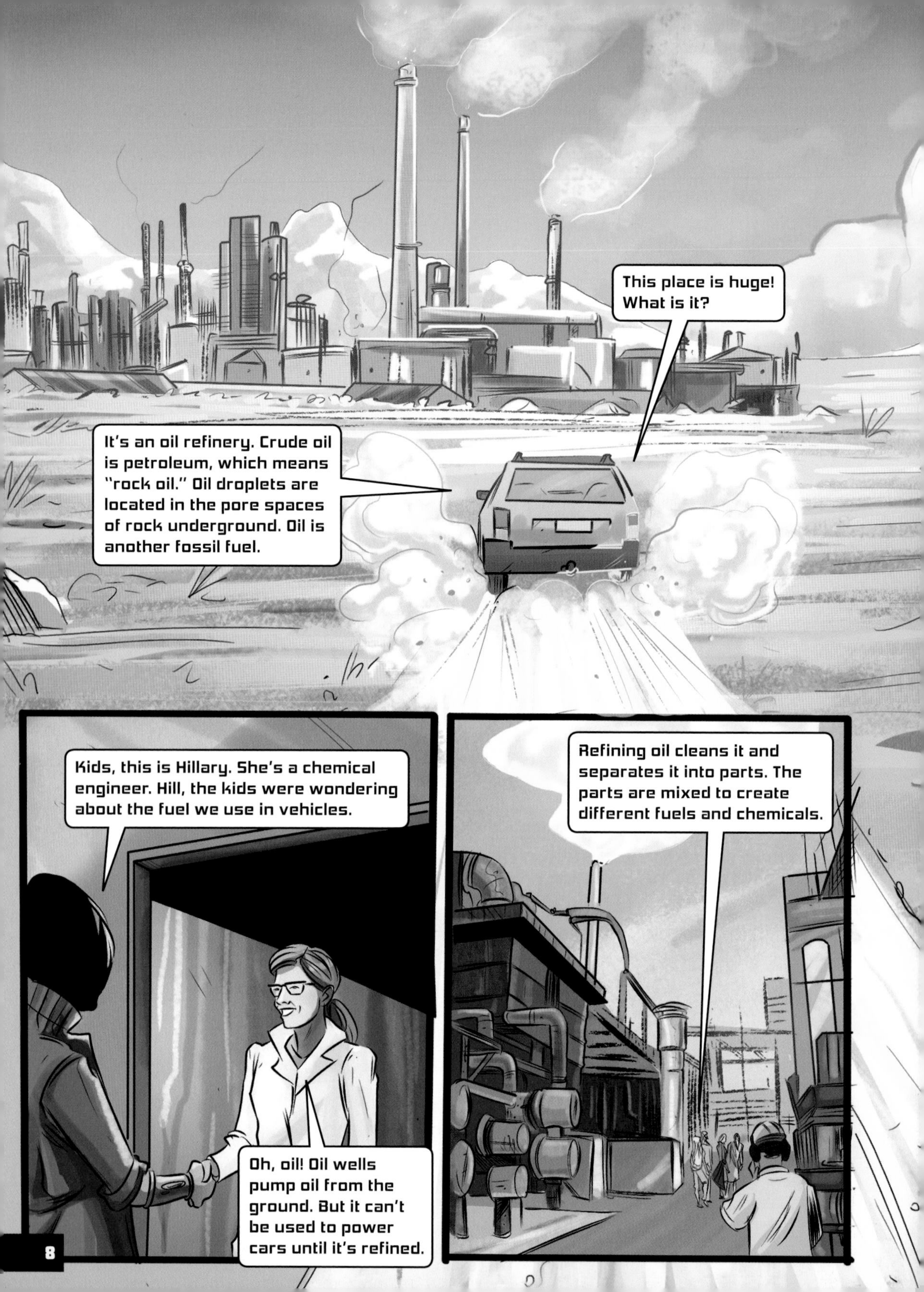
This place is huge! What is it?
It's an oil refinery. Crude oil is petroleum, which means "rock oil." Oil droplets are located in the pore spaces of rock underground. Oil is another fossil fuel.
Kids, this is Hillary. She's a chemical engineer. Hill, the kids were wondering about the fuel we use in vehicles.
Oh, oil! Oil wells pump oil from the ground. But it can't be used to power cars until it's refined.
Refining oil cleans it and separates it into parts. The parts are mixed to create different fuels and chemicals.

THE GREENHOUSE EFFECT ||||||||||||||

When sunlight hits the Earth, some of its energy is absorbed, and some is reflected back to space. Earth's atmosphere has a natural layer of greenhouse gases that traps some of this heat. Burning fossil fuels adds extra greenhouse gases to the atmosphere. Most scientists think that these additional gases are trapping more heat than necessary. This is called global warming. Man-made global warming can cause extreme weather patterns and change sea levels. The results could be disastrous

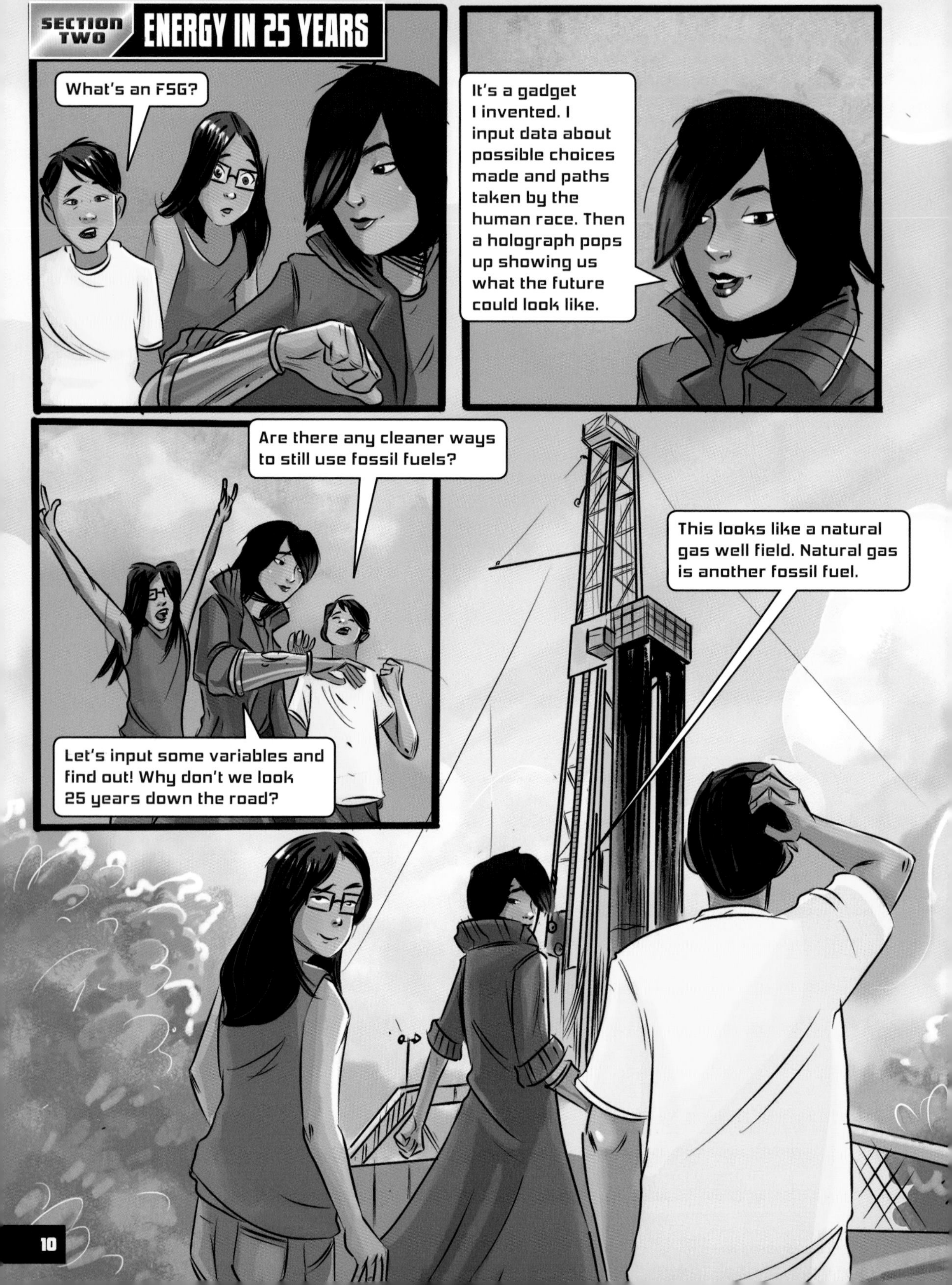
SECTION TWO
ENERGY IN 25 YEARS
What's an FSG?
It's a gadget I invented. I input data about possible choices made and paths taken by the human race. Then a holograph pops up showing us what the future could look like.
Are there any cleaner ways to still use fossil fuels?
Let's input some variables and find out! Why don't we look 25 years down the road?
This looks like a natural gas well field. Natural gas is another fossil fuel.

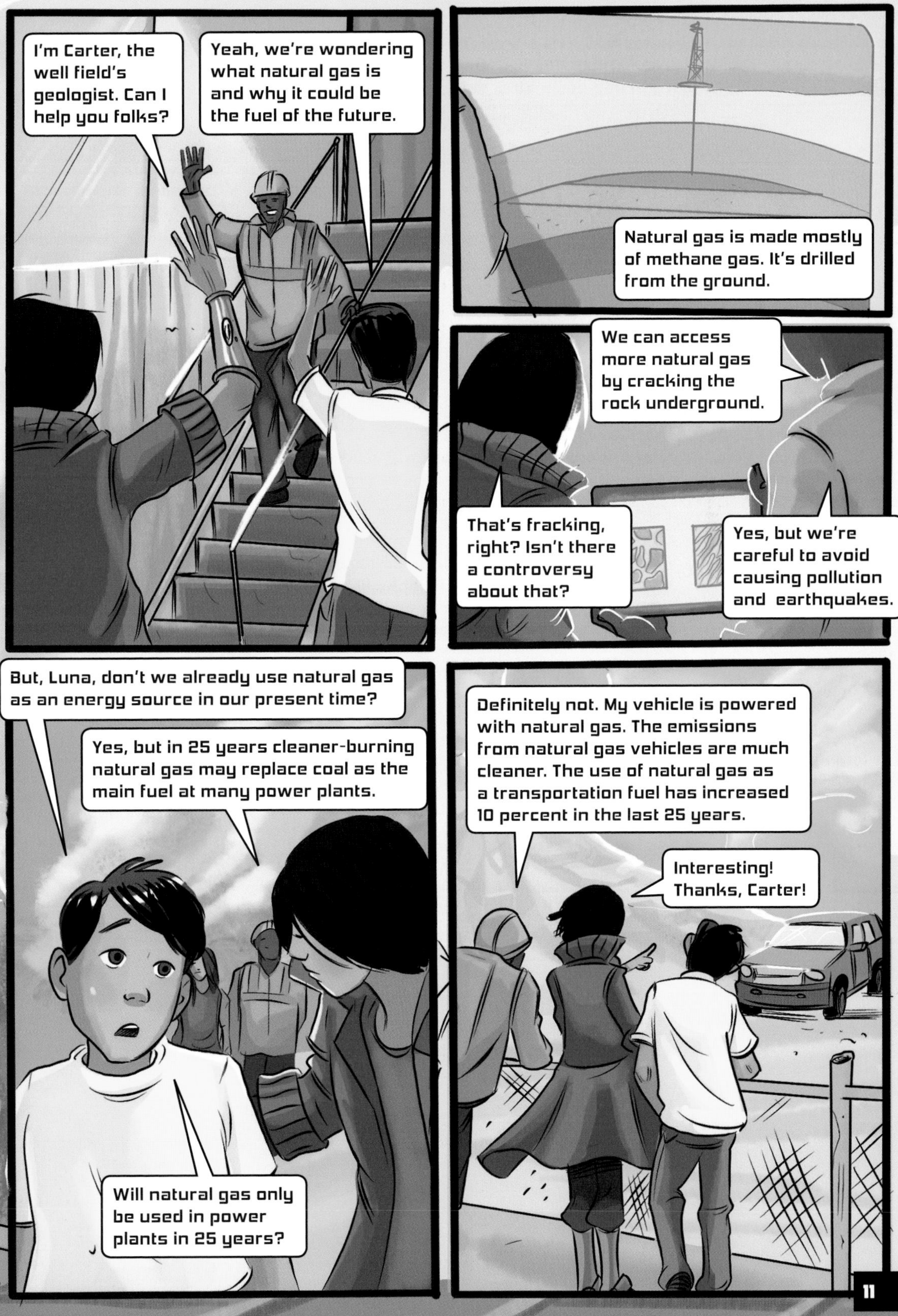
I'm Carter, the well field's geologist. Can I help you folks?
Yeah, we're wondering what natural gas is and why it could be the fuel of the future.
Natural gas is made mostly of methane gas. It's drilled from the ground.
We can access more natural gas by cracking the rock underground.
That's fracking, right? Isn't there a controversy about that?
Yes, but we're careful to avoid causing pollution and earthquakes.
But, Luna, don't we already use natural gas as an energy source in our present time?
Yes, but in 25 years cleaner-burning natural gas may replace coal as the main fuel at many power plants.
Will natural gas only be used in power plants in 25 years?
Definitely not. My vehicle is powered with natural gas. The emissions from natural gas vehicles are much cleaner. The use of natural gas as a transportation fuel has increased 10 percent in the last 25 years.
Interesting! Thanks, Carter!

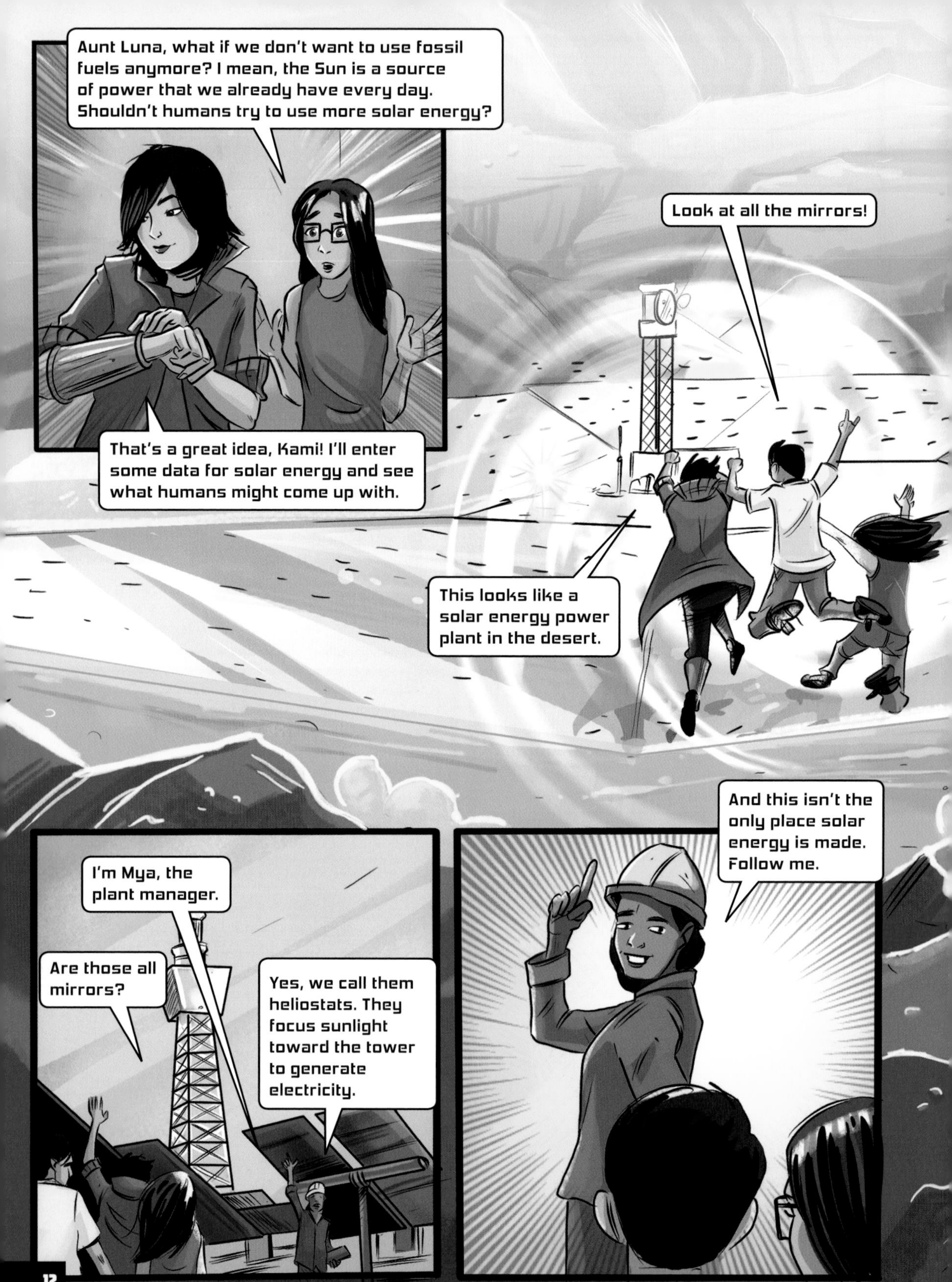
Aunt Luna, what if we don't want to use fossil fuels anymore? I mean, the Sun is a source of power that we already have every day. Shouldn't humans try to use more solar energy?
That's a great idea, Kami! I'll enter some data for solar energy and see what humans might come up with.
Look at all the mirrors!
This looks like a solar energy power plant in the desert.
I'm Mya, the plant manager.
Are those all mirrors?
Yes, we call them heliostats. They focus sunlight toward the tower to generate electricity.
And this isn't the only place solar energy is made. Follow me.

This is a solar neighborhood. All homes here generate some of their own electricity from these solar panels on the roofs.

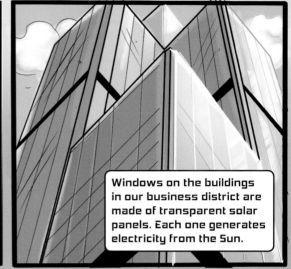

Windows on the buildings in our business district are made of transparent solar panels. Each one generates electricity from the Sun.

The parking lot and streets are made of solar panels, too. Of course, solar power is only generated when the parking spaces are vacant.

What do you do if snow covers the streets and parking lots?

Heaters can be installed in the solar panels to melt snow.

That's awesome!

Solar energy seems like the perfect clean energy source.

Well, it's not perfect. We always need a backup energy source for dark nights and cloudy days.

That makes sense. Thanks for the great information!

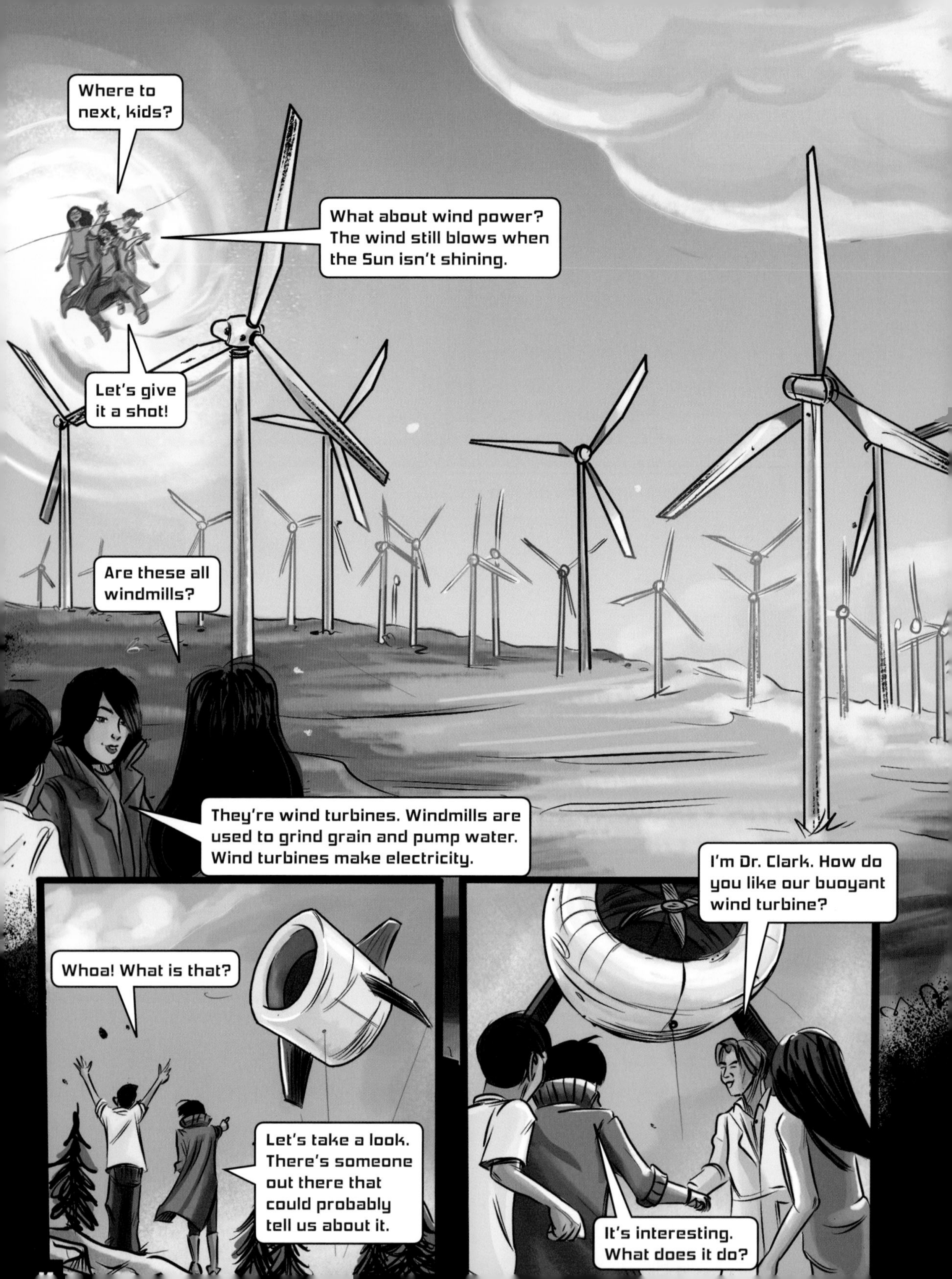
Where to next, kids?
What about wind power? The wind still blows when the Sun isn't shining.
Let's give it a shot!
Are these all windmills?
They're wind turbines. Windmills are used to grind grain and pump water. Wind turbines make electricity.
Whoa! What is that?
Let's take a look. There's someone out there that could probably tell us about it.
I'm Dr. Clark. How do you like our buoyant wind turbine?
It's interesting. What does it do?

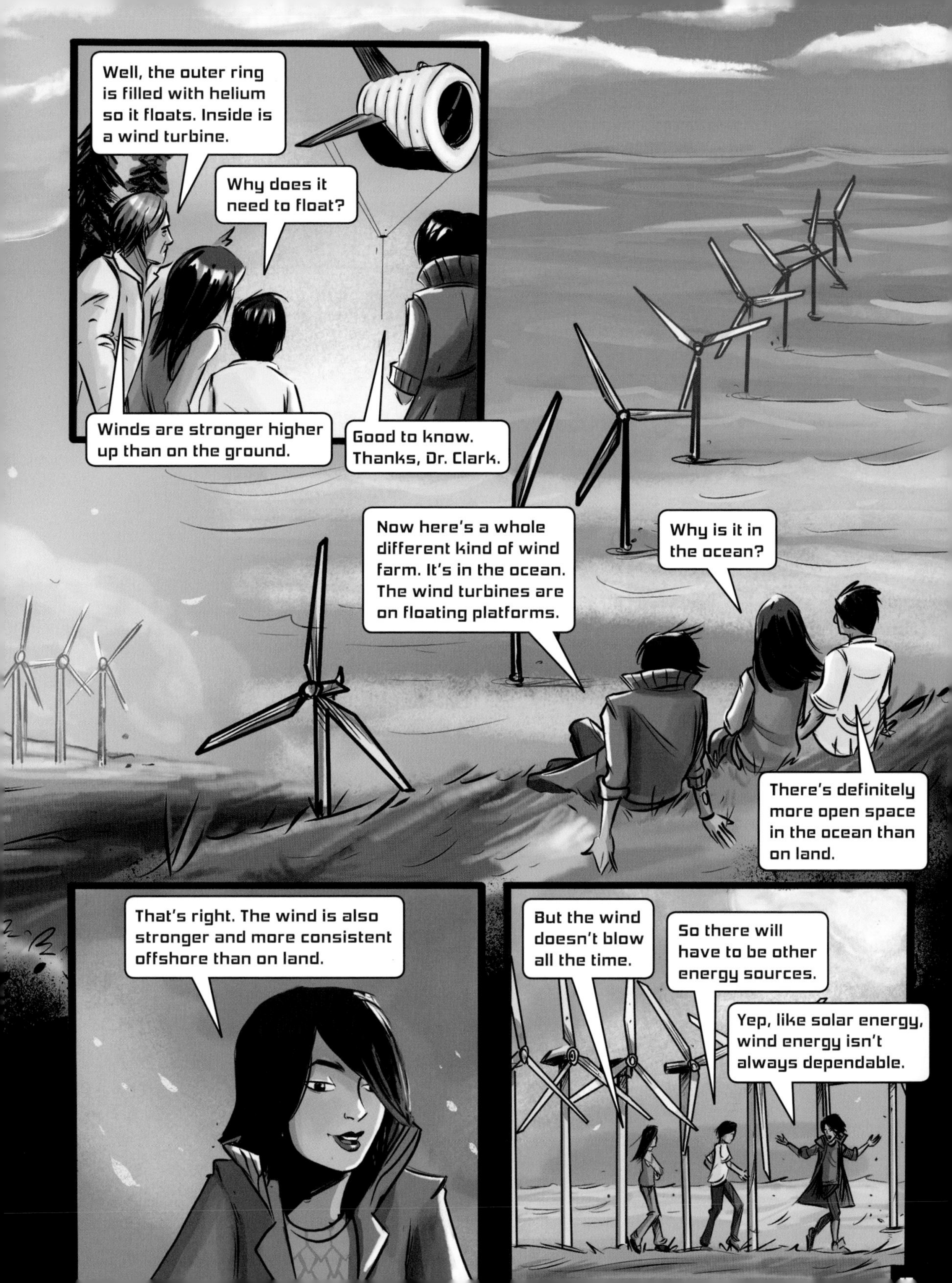
Well, the outer ring is filled with helium so it floats. Inside is a wind turbine.
Why does it need to float?
Winds are stronger higher up than on the ground.
Good to know. Thanks, Dr. Clark.
Now here's a whole different kind of wind farm. It's in the ocean. The wind turbines are on floating platforms.
Why is it in the ocean?
There's definitely more open space in the ocean than on land.
That's right. The wind is also stronger and more consistent offshore than on land.
But the wind doesn't blow all the time.
So there will have to be other energy sources.
Yep, like solar energy, wind energy isn't always dependable.

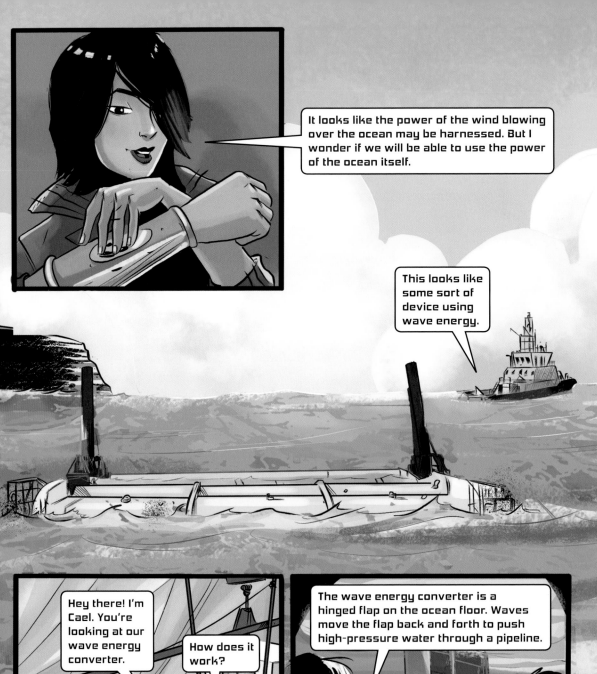

It looks like the power of the wind blowing over the ocean may be harnessed. But I wonder if we will be able to use the power of the ocean itself.

This looks like some sort of device using wave energy.

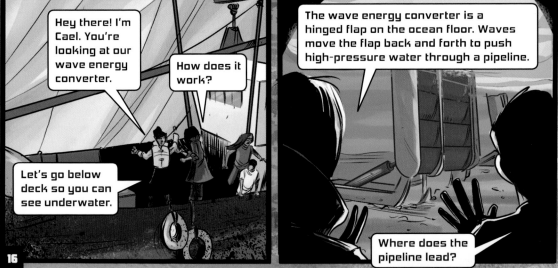

Hey there! I'm Cael. You're looking at our wave energy converter.

How does it work?

Let's go below deck so you can see underwater.

The wave energy converter is a hinged flap on the ocean floor. Waves move the flap back and forth to push high-pressure water through a pipeline.

Where does the pipeline lead?

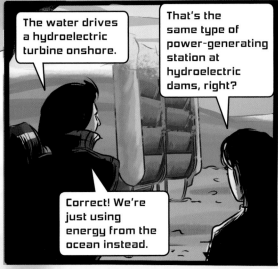

The water drives a hydroelectric turbine onshore.

That's the same type of power-generating station at hydroelectric dams, right?

Correct! We're just using energy from the ocean instead.

We have a wave farm too. It uses floating converters instead of submersible ones. Come on, I'll show you.

These look like giant sea snakes!

The joints of these long cylinders generate power as the waves move them up and down.

The good thing about wave energy is that it is renewable. Waves are always moving through the ocean and crashing on shore.

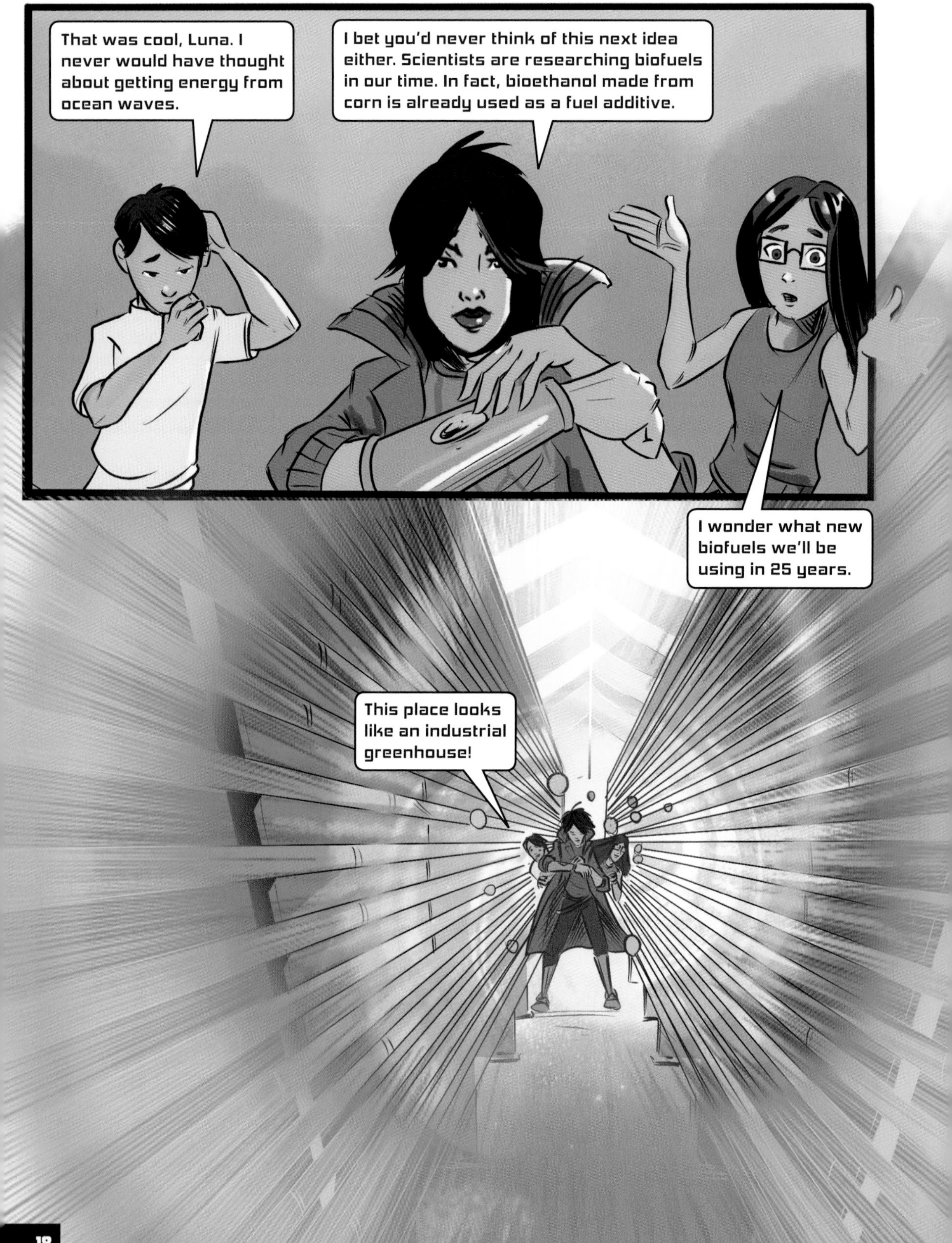
That was cool, Luna. I never would have thought about getting energy from ocean waves.
I bet you'd never think of this next idea either. Scientists are researching biofuels in our time. In fact, bioethanol made from corn is already used as a fuel additive.
I wonder what new biofuels we'll be using in 25 years.
This place looks like an industrial greenhouse!

Welcome to our photobioreactor. I'm Grace, the plant's microbiologist. These tubes grow algae for fuel.

Algae as fuel!?

Yep! In my time algae biofuel has replaced petroleum fuels. We use them in vehicles.

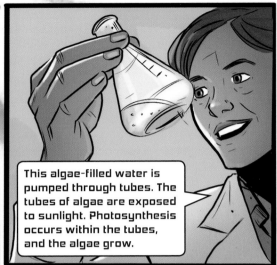

This algae-filled water is pumped through tubes. The tubes of algae are exposed to sunlight. Photosynthesis occurs within the tubes, and the algae grow.

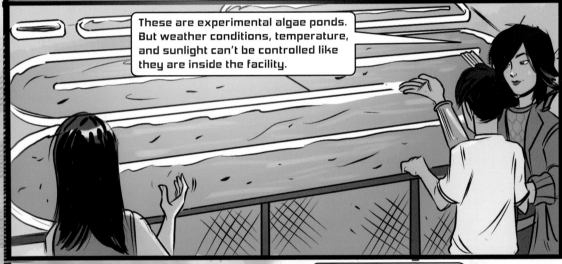

These are experimental algae ponds. But weather conditions, temperature, and sunlight can't be controlled like they are inside the facility.

I just don't see how you can get fuel from algae.

We harvest the algae and filter the water out. Next we squeeze out algae oil. Then we add a chemical that makes the algae release more oil.

So what's so great about using algae biofuels?

Algae is a renewable resource. It grows quickly. Biofuels have been made from corn and soybeans too, but using algae allows those crops to remain food crops.

SECTION THREE BY THE YEAR 2120

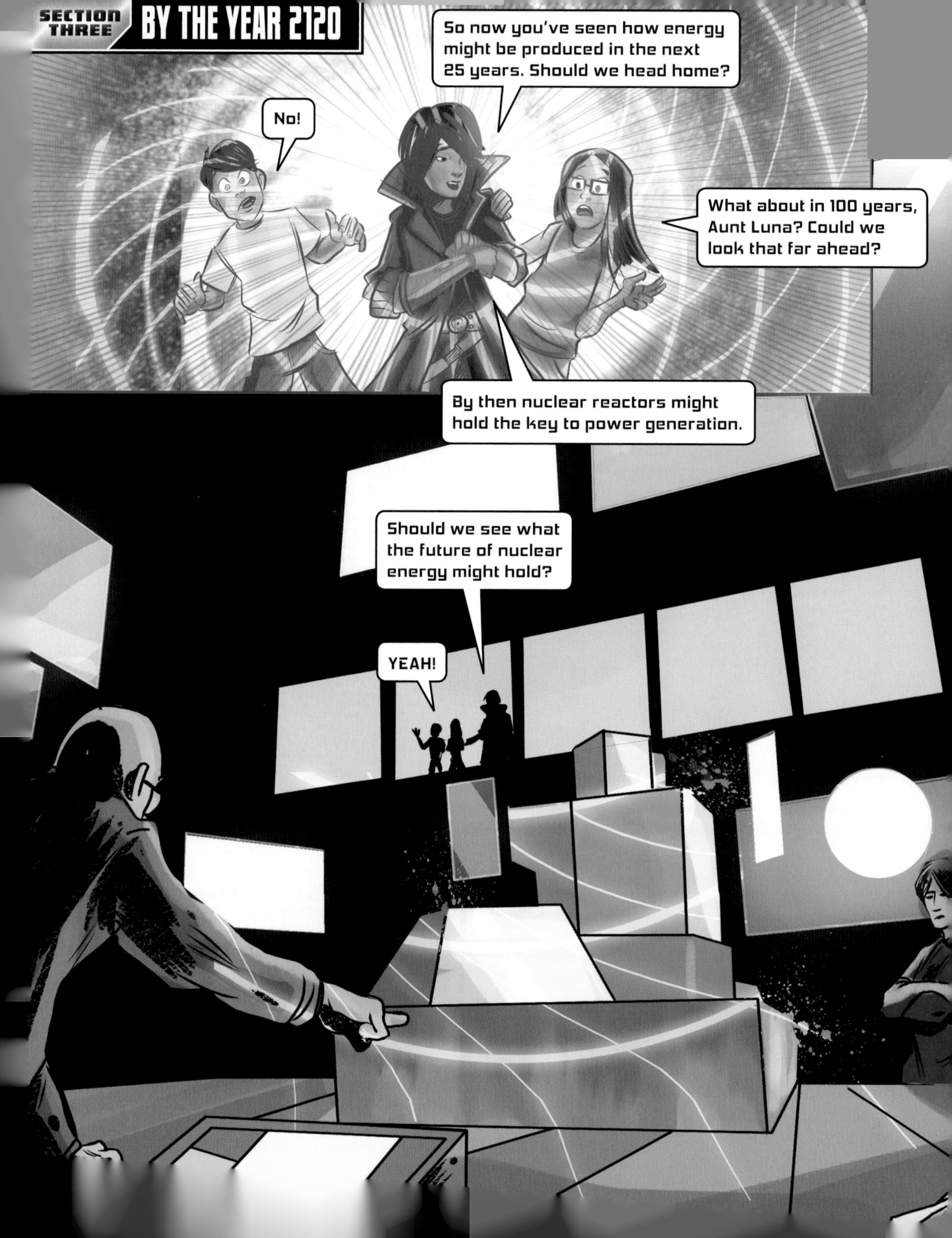

So now you've seen how energy might be produced in the next 25 years. Should we head home?
No!
What about in 100 years, Aunt Luna? Could we look that far ahead?
By then nuclear reactors might hold the key to power generation.
Should we see what the future of nuclear energy might hold?
YEAH!

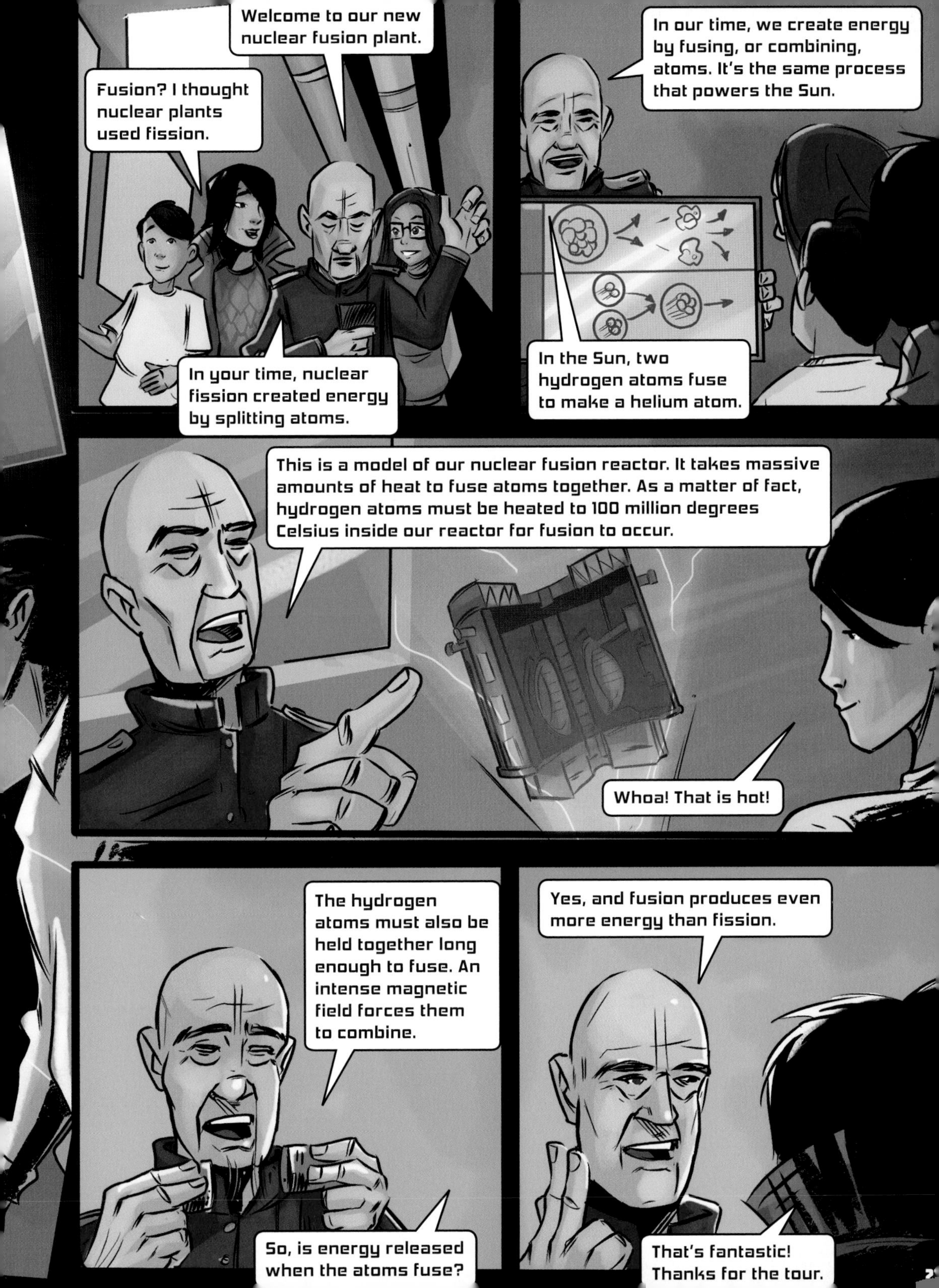
Welcome to our new nuclear fusion plant.
Fusion? I thought nuclear plants used fission.
In your time, nuclear fission created energy by splitting atoms.
In our time, we create energy by fusing, or combining, atoms. It's the same process that powers the Sun.
In the Sun, two hydrogen atoms fuse to make a helium atom.
This is a model of our nuclear fusion reactor. It takes massive amounts of heat to fuse atoms together. As a matter of fact, hydrogen atoms must be heated to 100 million degrees Celsius inside our reactor for fusion to occur.
Whoa! That is hot!
The hydrogen atoms must also be held together long enough to fuse. An intense magnetic field forces them to combine.
So, is energy released when the atoms fuse?
Yes, and fusion produces even more energy than fission.
That's fantastic! Thanks for the tour.

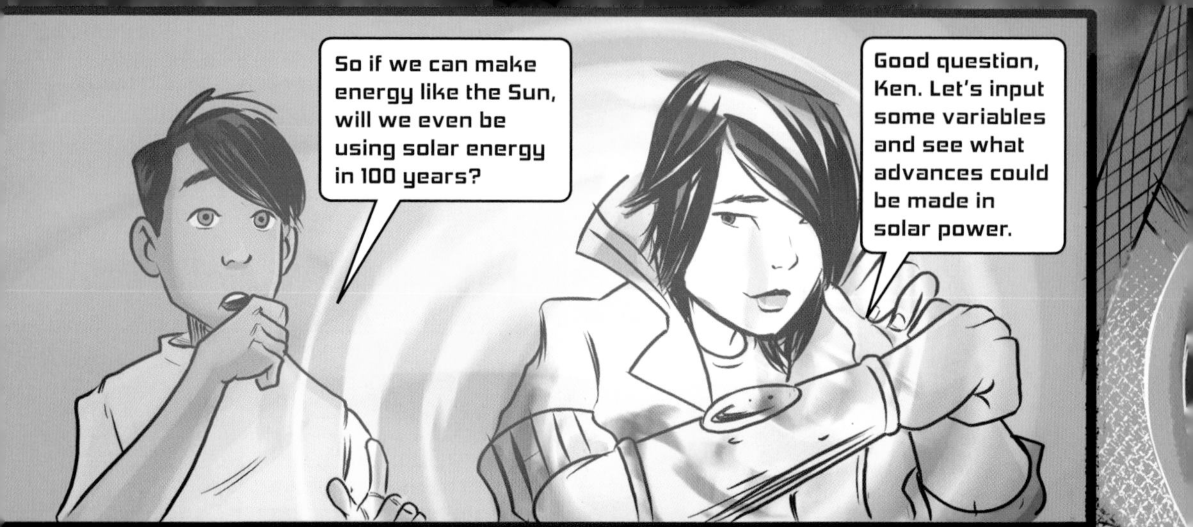
So if we can make energy like the Sun, will we even be using solar energy in 100 years?
Good question, Ken. Let's input some variables and see what advances could be made in solar power.

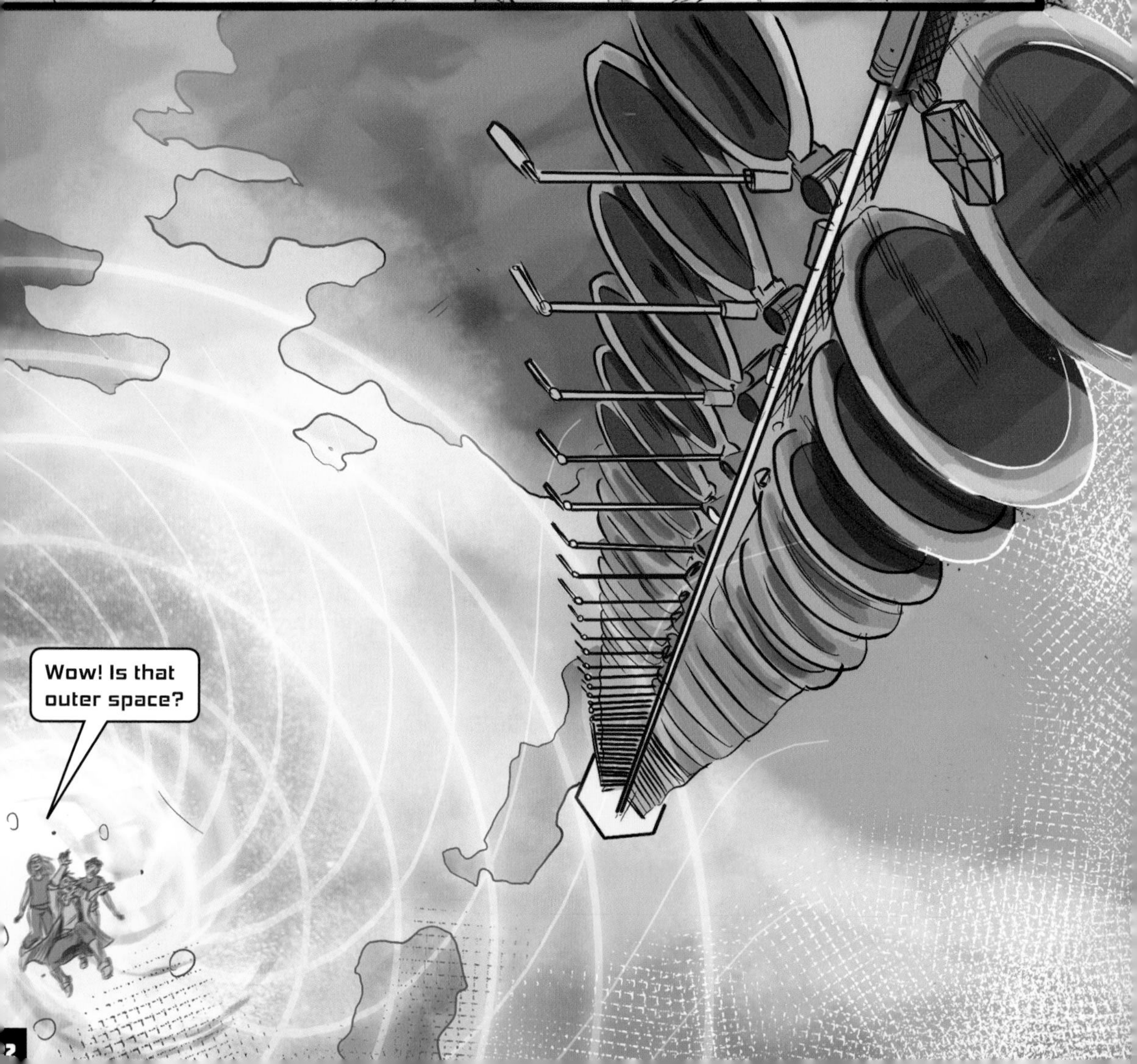
Wow! Is that outer space?

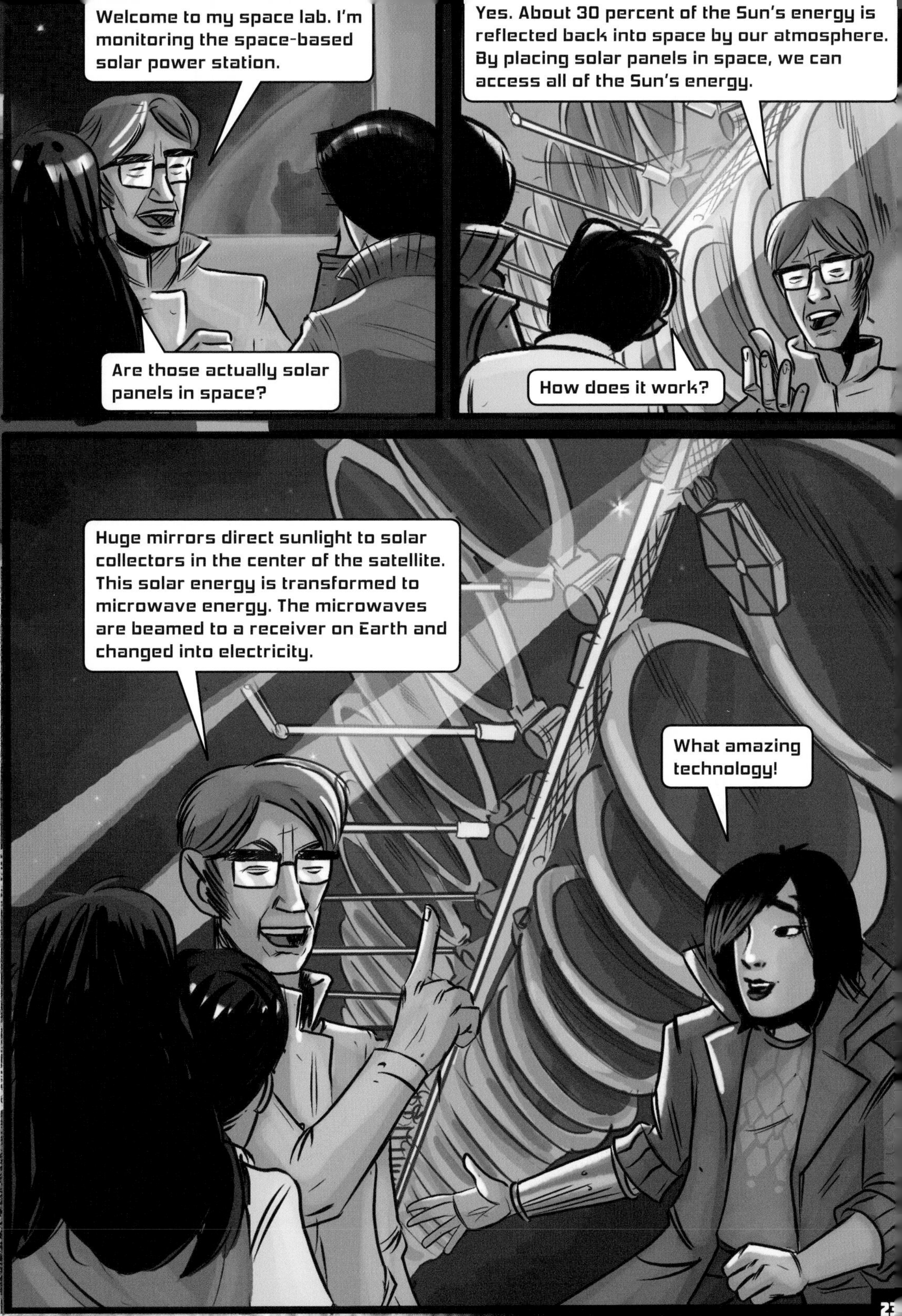
Welcome to my space lab. I'm monitoring the space-based solar power station.
Are those actually solar panels in space?
Yes. About 30 percent of the Sun's energy is reflected back into space by our atmosphere. By placing solar panels in space, we can access all of the Sun's energy.
How does it work?
Huge mirrors direct sunlight to solar collectors in the center of the satellite. This solar energy is transformed to microwave energy. The microwaves are beamed to a receiver on Earth and changed into electricity.
What amazing technology!

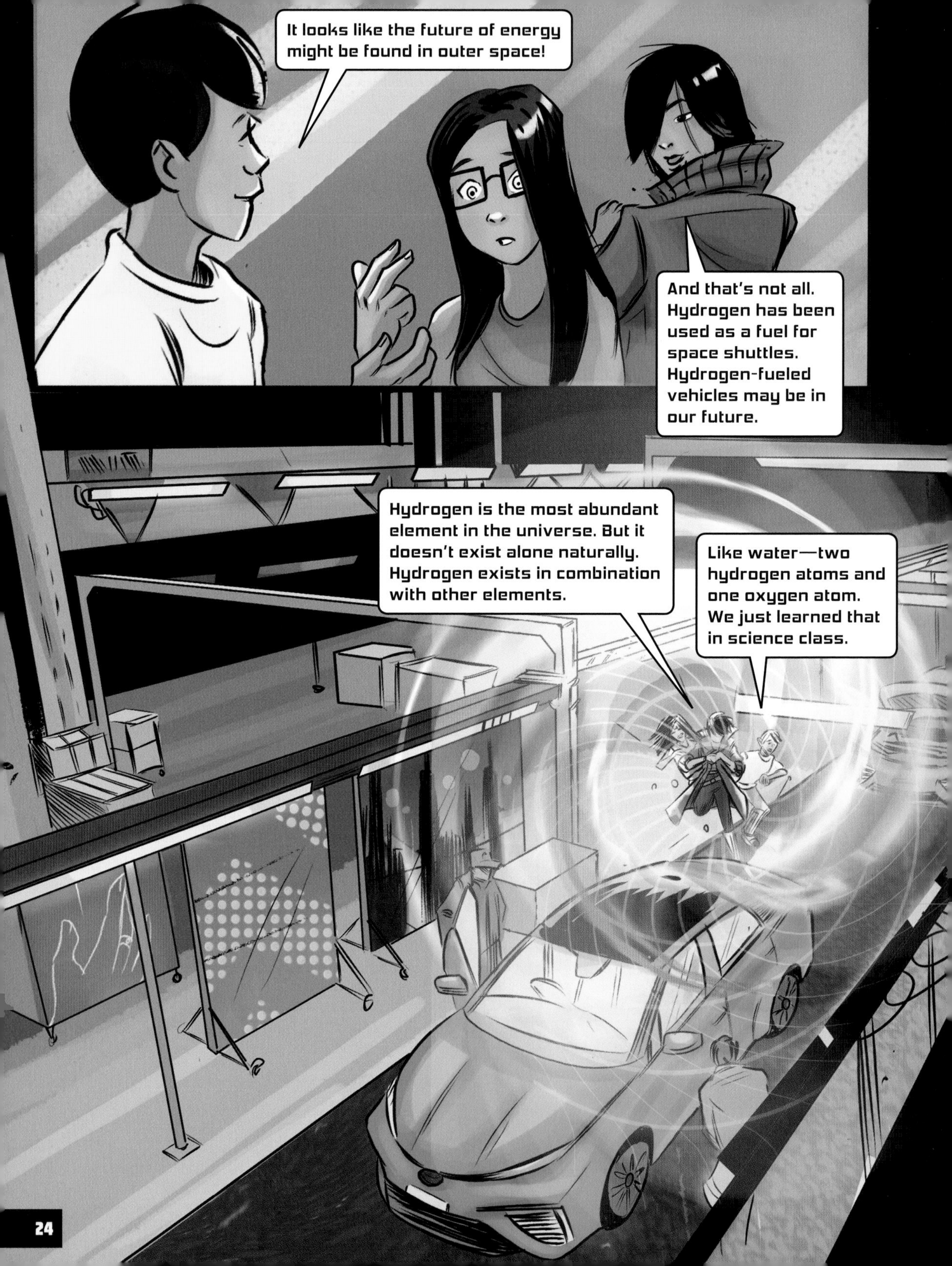
It looks like the future of energy might be found in outer space!
And that's not all. Hydrogen has been used as a fuel for space shuttles. Hydrogen-fueled vehicles may be in our future.
Hydrogen is the most abundant element in the universe. But it doesn't exist alone naturally. Hydrogen exists in combination with other elements.
Like water—two hydrogen atoms and one oxygen atom. We just learned that in science class.

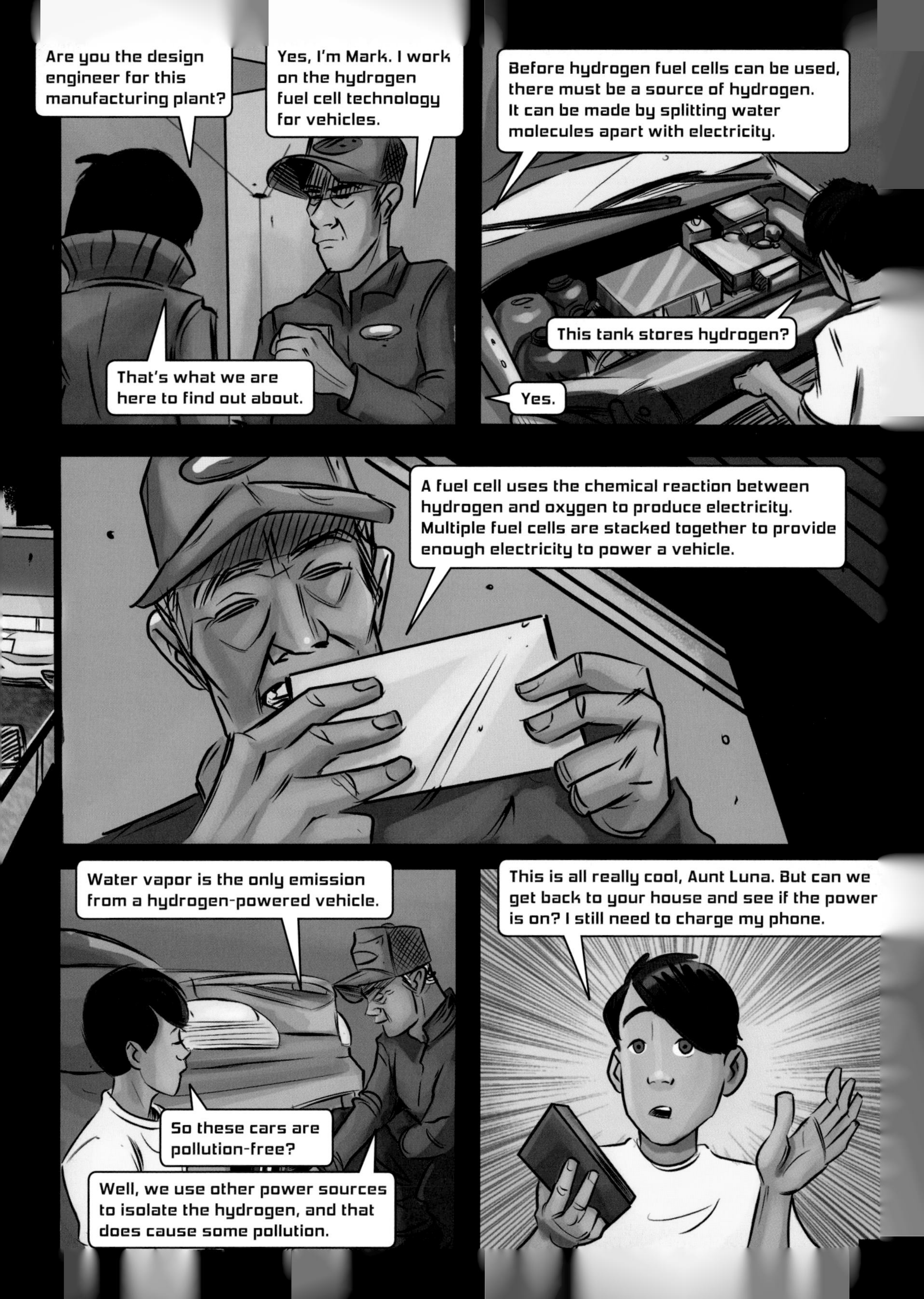
Are you the design engineer for this manufacturing plant?
Yes, I'm Mark. I work on the hydrogen fuel cell technology for vehicles.
That's what we are here to find out about.
Before hydrogen fuel cells can be used, there must be a source of hydrogen. It can be made by splitting water molecules apart with electricity.
This tank stores hydrogen?
Yes.
A fuel cell uses the chemical reaction between hydrogen and oxygen to produce electricity. Multiple fuel cells are stacked together to provide enough electricity to power a vehicle.
Water vapor is the only emission from a hydrogen-powered vehicle.
So these cars are pollution-free?
Well, we use other power sources to isolate the hydrogen, and that does cause some pollution.
This is all really cool, Aunt Luna. But can we get back to your house and see if the power is on? I still need to charge my phone.

SECTION FOUR POWER UP

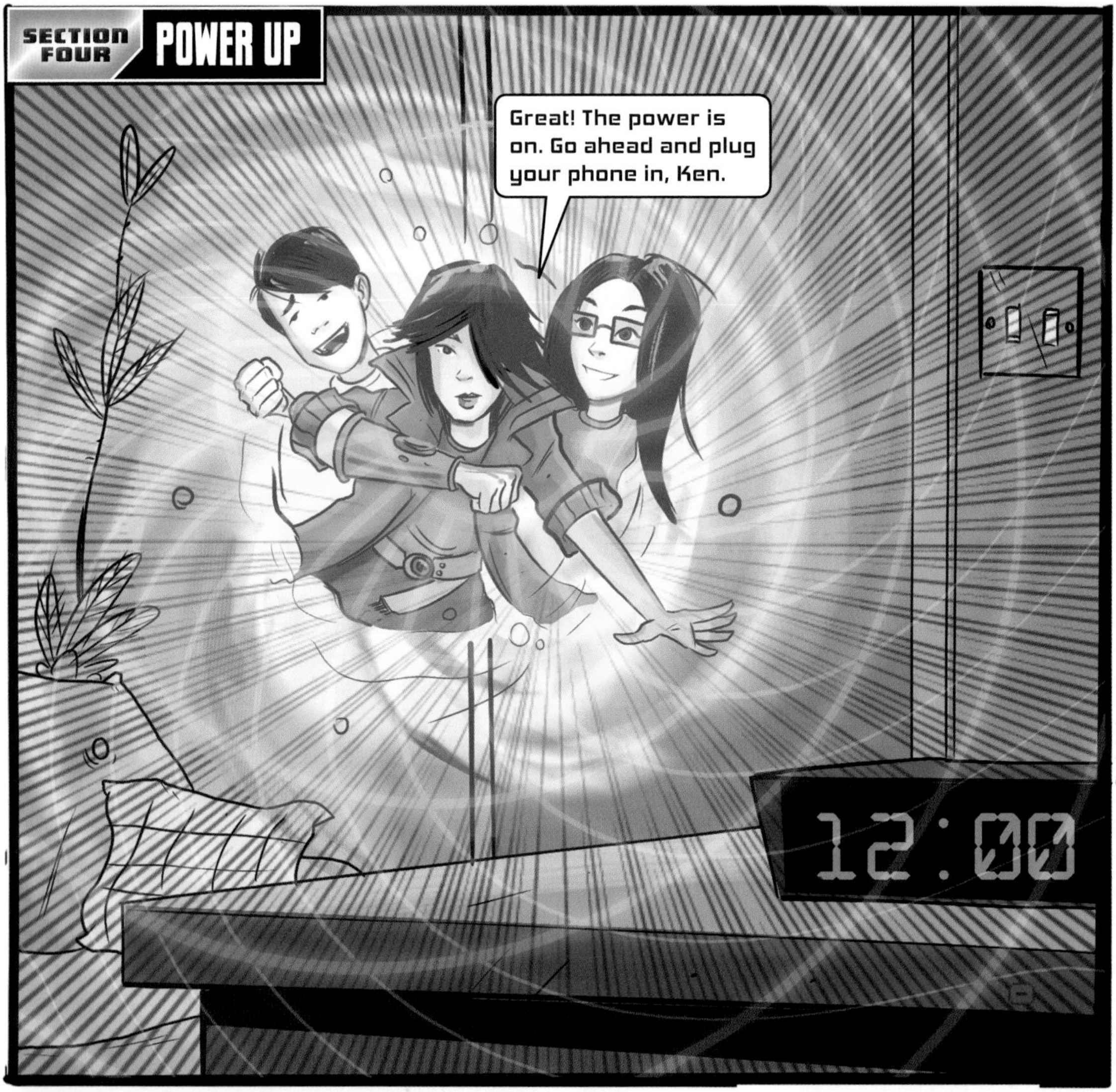

Great! The power is on. Go ahead and plug your phone in, Ken.

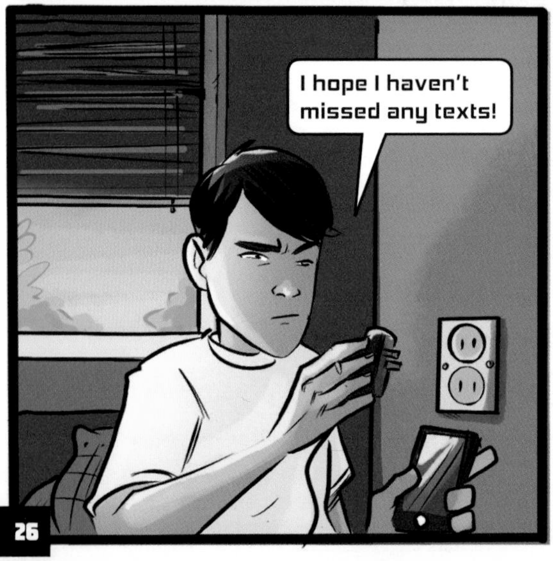

I hope I haven't missed any texts!

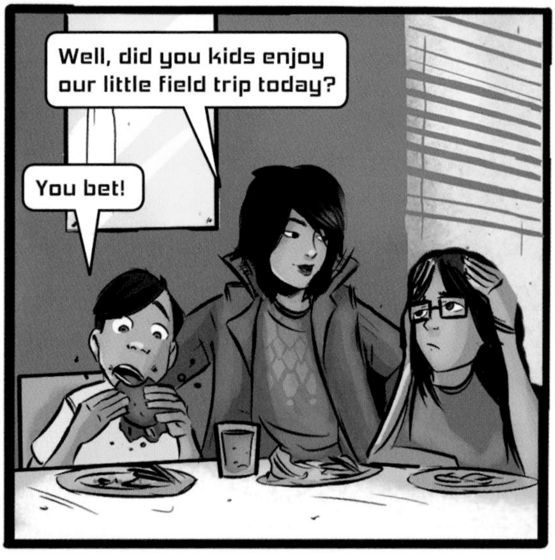

Well, did you kids enjoy our little field trip today?
You bet!

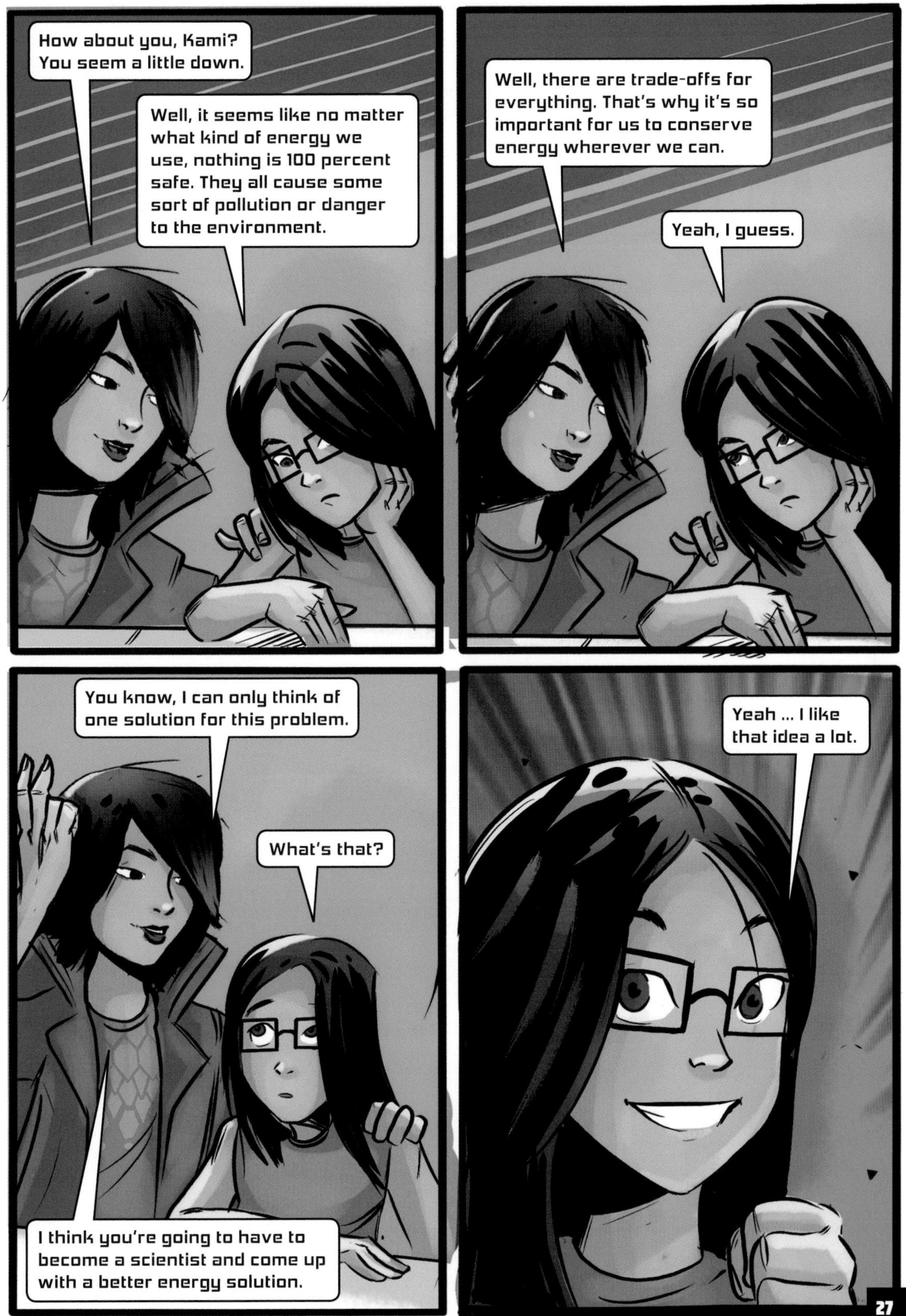
How about you, Kami? You seem a little down.
Well, it seems like no matter what kind of energy we use, nothing is 100 percent safe. They all cause some sort of pollution or danger to the environment.
Well, there are trade-offs for everything. That's why it's so important for us to conserve energy wherever we can.
Yeah, I guess.
You know, I can only think of one solution for this problem.
What's that?
I think you're going to have to become a scientist and come up with a better energy solution.
Yeah ... I like that idea a lot.

ENERGY AND THE FUTURE

- In 1859 the first oil well was drilled by Edwin L. Drake in Titusville, Pennsylvania, for the Seneca Oil Company.

- Coal is made mostly of carbon. Impurities, such as sulfur, are found naturally in coal. When coal is burned at power plants, sulfur combines with oxygen. This forms sulfur dioxide. The Environmental Protection Agency limits the amount of sulfur dioxide that power plants can release into the air. Power plants install devices called scrubbers to remove or "scrub" pollutants such as sulfur dioxide from their exhausts.

- In 2013 the total amount of energy *produced* in the United States can be broken down into the following percentages: natural gas (34.8%), coal (24.4%), oil (19.3%), renewable (11.4%), nuclear (10.1%).

- In 2013 the total amount of energy *consumed* in the United States can be broken down into the following percentages: petroleum (36%), natural gas (27%), coal (19%), renewable (10%), and nuclear (8%).

- Geothermal energy comes from heat in the Earth's core. Steam or hot water is piped through wells to the surface to turn turbines. This generates electricity. In 2013 geothermal power plants produced 0.4% of the energy produced in the United States. California produced 78% of this geothermal energy.

Natural gas is odorless. The strong "rotten egg" smell comes from a chemical that is added before the gas is distributed. The smell makes it easier to detect a leak.

Ocean waves contain kinetic energy, which is energy of motion. One power generator uses the up-and-down wave motion to force air in and out of a chamber. The air movement spins a turbine, generating electricity.

MORE ABOUT LUNA LI

Futurists are scientists who systematically study and explore possibilities about the future of human society and life on Earth. Luna proved herself to be brilliant in this field at a young age. She excelled in STEM subjects and earned her PhD in Alternative Futures from the University of Hawaii at Manoa. Luna invented a gadget she calls the Future Scenario Generator (FSG) that she wears on her wrist. Luna inputs current and predicted data into the FSG. It then crunches the numbers and creates a portal to a holographic reality that humans can enter and interact with.

coal (KOHL)—a black mineral formed from the remains of ancient plants; coal is mined underground and is burned as a fuel

crude oil (KROOD OYL)—a thick, black substance drilled from the Earth and used to make fuels such as gasoline and natural gas

fossil fuel (FAH-suhl FYOOL)—natural fuel formed from the remains of plants and animals; coal, oil, and natural gas are fossil fuels

generator (JEN-uh-ray-tur)—a machine that produces electricity by turning a magnet inside a coil of wire

global warming (GLOH-buhl WAR-ming)—an apparent gradual rise in the temperature of the Earth's atmosphere caused by the greenhouse effect

greenhouse gases (GREEN-houss GASS-ez)—gases such as carbon dioxide and methane that are found in the Earth's atmosphere and help hold heat in

power plant (POU-ur PLANT)—a building or group of buildings used to create electricity

refinery (ri-FYE-nuh-ree)—a place where petroleum is made into gasoline, motor oil, and other products

turbine (TUR-bine)—an engine powered by steam or gas; the steam or gas moves through the blades of a fanlike device and makes it turn

Mulder, Michelle. *Brilliant!: Shining a Light on Sustainable Energy.* Orca Footprints. Victoria, BC, Canada: Orca Book Publishers, 2013.

Ollhoff, Jim. *Fossil Fuels.* Future Energy. Minneapolis: ABDO Publishing Company, 2010.

Spilsbury, Richard, and Louise Spilsbury. *Energy.* Essential Physical Science. Chicago: Capstone Heinemann Library, 2014.

Zuchora-Walske, Christine. *Energy in the Real World.* Minneapolis: ABDO Publishing Company, 2013.

INTERNET SITES

FactHound offers a safe, fun way to find Internet sites related to this book. All sites on FactHound have been researched by our staff.

Here's all you do:

Visit *www.facthound.com*

Type in this code: 9781491482674

Super-cool stuff!

Check out projects, games and lots more at
www.capstonekids.com